By **HEATHER CAMLOT**

Illustrated by **VICTOR WONG**

BECOMING BIONIC

and Other Ways Science Is Making Us Super

Owlkids Books

For my mom and dad, the greatest superheroes I know —H.C.

Hi, Mom! Hi, Dad! —V.W.

ACKNOWLEDGMENTS

A huge thank-you to Mitchell Brown, for debating what it means to be a superhero and sharing his comic book knowledge; to Dr. Jonathan Fridell, for reminding me that immortality can also come through organ donation and being remembered by others, as well as for his medical and superhero input; to Stacey Roderick, for being my real-life WordGirl and super-extraordinary editor; and to the entire Owlkids Books team, for making me feel more super than I am.

Text © 2023 Heather Camlot | Illustrations © 2023 Victor Wong

Owlkids Books acknowledges the financial support of the Canada Council for the Arts, the Ontario Arts Council, the Government of Canada through the Canada Book Fund (CBF) and the Government of Ontario through the Ontario Creates Book Initiative for our publishing activities.

Owlkids Books gratefully acknowledges that our office in Toronto is located on the traditional territory of many nations, including the Mississaugas of the Credit, the Chippewa, the Wendat, the Anishinaabeg, and the Haudenosaunee Peoples.

Published in Canada by Owlkids Books Inc., 1 Eglinton Avenue East, Toronto, ON M4P 3A1
Published in the US by Owlkids Books Inc., 1700 Fourth Street, Berkeley, CA 94710

Library of Congress Control Number: 2022939170

Library and Archives Canada Cataloguing in Publication

Title: Becoming bionic, and other ways science is making us super / written
   by Heather Camlot ; illustrated by Victor Wong.
Names: Camlot, Heather, author. | Wong, Victor (Illustrator), illustrator.
Description: Includes bibliographical references.
Identifiers: Canadiana 20220254265 | ISBN 9781771474610 (hardcover)
Subjects: LCSH: Human body and technology—Juvenile literature. | LCSH:
   Human body and technology—History—Juvenile literature. | LCSH:
   Human body and technology—Moral and ethical aspects—Juvenile
   literature. | LCSH: Technological innovations—Jvenile literature. | LCSH:
   Inventions—Juvenile literature. | LCSH: Science—Juvenile literature.
Classification: LCC T14.5 .C35 2023 | DDC j303.48/3—dc23

Edited by Stacey Roderick | Designed by Alisa Baldwin

Manufactured in Guangdong Province, Dongguan City, China, in September 2022, by Toppan Leefung Packaging & Printing (Dongguan) Co., Ltd. Job #BAYDC113

A   B   C   D   E   F

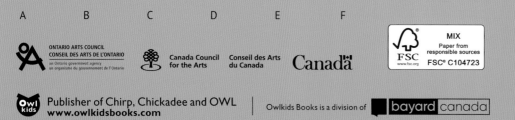

Publisher of Chirp, Chickadee and OWL
www.owlkidsbooks.com

Owlkids Books is a division of bayard canada

CONTENTS

POWER UP!

If you could have any superpower, what would it be?

Would you want to regenerate like Wolverine? Fly like Shazam? Turn invisible like Violet Parr? Be crazy strong like the Hulk? Control minds like the Scarlet Witch? Or be immortal like Klaus Hargreeves?

Too bad humans can't actually do any of these things ... or can we?

The fact is, scientists are constantly searching for new ways to extend human capabilities. And to do this, they are applying their expertise in a whole range of fields, from bionics (the science of designing prostheses modeled on biological parts) to psychology (the study of the mind and behavior). Believe it or not, many of the imaginary superpowers we see in comics and movies and on television are already a reality—and even more are on their way!

In this book, you'll be introduced to some incredible scientific inventions and advancements that can push us past the limits of the bodies we were born with. In each section, you'll travel back in time to discover some early superpowered ideas before zapping ahead to today's science, then finally blasting forward to learn what the future might have in store. Along the way, you may just be inspired to dream up your own superhero innovations to help us live our best and longest lives.

– SECTION 1 –
SUPER PARTS

Wolverine can rebuild himself from a single drop of blood. Ms. Marvel can take a bullet and keep on ticking by reverting to her non-superhero form. Deadpool can slice off his hand and grow it back in no time.

This ability to regrow a body part that has been damaged or removed is called regeneration. Humans can't regenerate an entire arm or leg like certain superheroes can, but we can regrow part of our liver and the tip of a finger. It's a start, right? That's certainly what the scientists who are exploring the possibilities of regeneration think.

Some superheroes who can't regenerate have a different super-powerful resource at their disposal: high-tech prostheses. Prostheses are artificial body parts, and in the superhero world, these replacements are usually super-powered versions of biological parts. When Blade had to bite off his hand to escape being chained up, he's given a gun-like attachment and later a cybernetic hand. Then there's Aquaman's cybernetic golden harpoon, which replaced his left hand after it was devoured by piranhas. (In the superhero world, the word "cybernetic" basically means combining body and machine. Cybernetic + organism = cyborg.)

When it comes to real-world prostheses, we think most often of artificial arms and legs. But there are many other kinds, including artificial eyes, ears, noses, teeth, and heart valves. Some of these prostheses may not have the full capability of a biological part, but scientific advancements are making many replacements closer to the real thing—and even going beyond what nature intended.

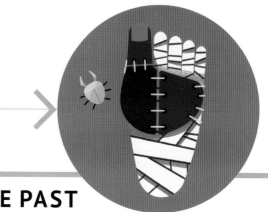

950 to 710 BCE: Made of leather and wood, the Cairo toe is considered the earliest working prosthesis. Attached to a female mummy discovered in a burial chamber outside Luxor, Egypt, the toe not only looks good but can also bend.

Timeline: INVENTIVE PARTS FROM THE PAST

Give Me a Hand

We don't know when the very first prosthesis was made, but we can assume it helped its wearer overcome the physical challenges and possible psychological issues, such as depression and anxiety, that can happen after someone loses a limb.

Circa 1820: The Anglesey leg is created by James Potts for the Marquess of Anglesey, who lost a limb during the Battle of Waterloo. Made from lime wood and leather, this prosthetic leg has a hinged knee and ankle that use cat gut (which is actually sheep intestine) for tendons so they work together for better movement.

1861: Eighteen-year-old James Hanger becomes the American Civil War's first amputee when he is hit in the leg by a cannonball just two days after enlisting. Once back home, he whittles an artificial leg out of slats of wood from a barrel, then adds a hinged knee and ankle. He goes on to create prostheses for other soldiers and establishes an international prosthetic company that still exists today.

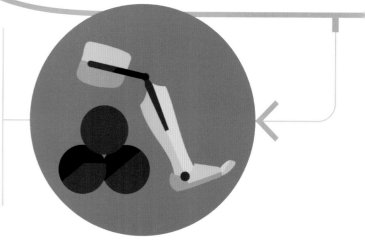

300 BCE: The Capua leg is found in a grave in Capua, Italy. This earliest known prosthetic leg is from the era when medical practitioners learned how to stop bleeding, which makes amputation a less deadly treatment. Unfortunately, the bronze and wooden leg is accidentally destroyed by a bomb in the Second World War.

Circa 1550: Designed by a French military surgeon named Ambroise Paré and worn by an army captain, le Petit Lorrain is a mechanical hand that uses catches and springs so the wearer can open and close his fingers. Dr. Paré begins making prostheses after learning that some amputee patients are taking their own lives. He believes his devices will improve patients' physical and mental well-being. He even shares his designs and instructions so others can make them, too.

Circa 1920: As wounded soldiers come home from the First World War, the need for artificial limbs skyrockets. Veterans require new innovations so they can return to work. The McKay heavy working arm features a lightweight hand with exchangeable attachments, such as a hook, chisel holder, and hammer.

2012: Scientists show just how far prostheses have come when they use twenty-eight parts—including arms, legs, a heart, lungs, eyes, ears, and an eerily lifelike face—to create the world's first "bionic man." This robot can walk and talk and has pumping blood. He's still missing a few key parts, such as a stomach and a liver, but he's proof that about two-thirds of the human body can be replaced. And at $1 million, this bionic man costs a fraction of what it took to rebuild Colonel Steve Austin in the 1970s TV show *The Six Million Dollar Man.*

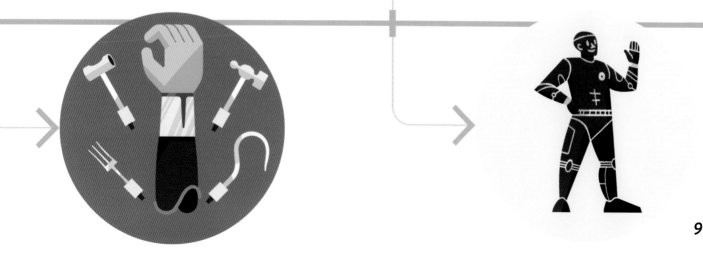

Becoming Bionic

Today's prostheses have come a long way. They provide better fit and comfort, are stronger and lighter, and offer more control and movement.

MIND OVER MATTER

Researchers are revolutionizing prostheses by harnessing the power of the brain! By simply thinking about what you want it to do, your prosthesis will do it—much like a biological limb would. One new approach involves wrapping tiny muscle grafts (healthy muscle taken from another part of the body) around a residual limb's nerve endings to strengthen the signals coming from the nerves. Electrodes in the muscle pick up the brain's commands to control the prosthesis. Another device in development uses artificial intelligence (AI) to read nerve signals through your skin. Just slip on the prosthesis—no surgery needed. Scientists aren't just trying to improve how a prosthesis moves— they're working to help the brain interpret what a prosthesis *feels*, such as heat or cold, pain, and texture.

PUT IT IN PRINT

A traditionally made prosthetic arm can cost tens of thousands of dollars— pretty pricey, especially when it's for a kid who will soon grow out of it. With 3D printing, a prosthetic arm can be made for as little as a hundred dollars. Prostheses can also be more lightweight, making them more comfortable for smaller bodies and easier to use. And the limbs can be designed to reflect hobbies and passions—favorite colors, characters, video games . . . you name it. In 2015, one boy received a replica Iron Man prosthetic arm—personally delivered by actor Robert Downey Jr., who plays Iron Man in the movies!

ATHLETIC PROSTHESES

Competition is fierce for the athletes in the Paralympics, the Invictus Games, and the X Games. And whatever the sport, there are specialized prostheses for every participant's needs. Like what? Upper limb clips that can hold a kayak paddle. Legs that flex and extend for downhill skiing. Metal sleeves that slip over a golf club handle. A flexible, curved hand for playing basketball. Skate attachments for playing ice hockey. And so many more!

1980

Materials:
Steel and fiberglass leg; wooden and rubber foot, covered by a sneaker

Knee:
Steel hinge-like joint and elastic strapping

Fit:
Socket, suction, and belts

Shock absorption:
None—requires user to burn a lot of energy

Weight:
About 4 kg (9 lb.)

A Leg Up

On April 12, 1980, three years after losing his right leg to cancer, twenty-one-year-old Terry Fox set out on his Marathon of Hope to raise money for cancer research. He was forced to end his marathon after completing 5,373 km (3,339 mi.) of his 8,500 km (5,282 mi.) cross-Canada run when the cancer returned. Sadly, he died soon after, on June 28, 1981.

Terry's leg was much different from a running prosthesis used today:

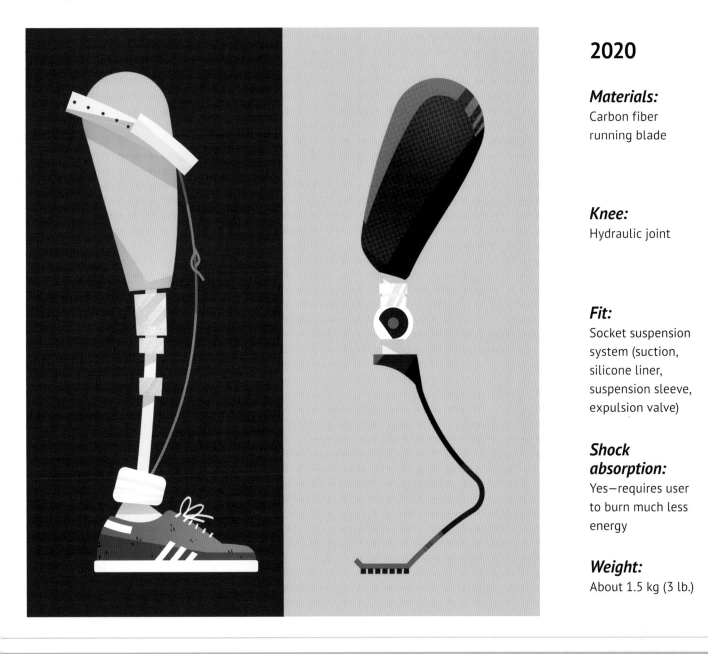

2020

Materials:
Carbon fiber running blade

Knee:
Hydraulic joint

Fit:
Socket suspension system (suction, silicone liner, suspension sleeve, expulsion valve)

Shock absorption:
Yes—requires user to burn much less energy

Weight:
About 1.5 kg (3 lb.)

Making a Comeback

When it comes to regeneration, humans are ... well, only human. Although a few of our body parts will regrow naturally, some scientists are trying to take that regeneration to a superhuman level. Others are looking to the animal world to uncover the genetic secrets of super-regenerators.

LEAPING LIVERS

The human liver is pretty darn cool. Even if as much as 50 percent of it is damaged, healthy hepatocyte cells (special cells found only in the liver) can multiply and regrow the tissue, sometimes in as little as thirty days! When a liver is more damaged, surgeons can perform a partial transplant using part of the organ from a living donor—and *both* the donor's and the patient's liver will regenerate! Scientists are also working on growing livers in labs and on recycling unhealthy donor livers by washing out the original cells and replacing them with healthy ones.

GET UNDER ONE'S SKIN

Skin, our body's biggest organ, repairs itself with special cells called stem cells. But why does our skin tend to heal completely from paper cuts but scar from burns and more serious cuts? It depends on how deep the wound is and how the stem cells are activated. Researchers in Calgary, Alberta, say wounds have different "microenvironments": one is a regenerative zone, another a scar-forming zone. The first zone triggers genes inside the stem cells to develop skin so the wounded area will look as good as new. But in the second zone, different genes quickly close the skin to prevent infection. That's what leaves a scar. Researchers believe it will one day be possible to develop drugs to change those microenvironments from scar-making to skin-regenerating.

TIPPING POINT

A fingernail grows back, so why can't a fingertip? It can—as long as most of the nail and tissue below it are intact. In fact, there's a whole host of self-renewing stem cells under the base of your nails. These particular stem cells use signals carried by special proteins—molecules in your body—to help bone, skin, muscle, and nerves grow back. If the signal isn't activated because too much of the tissue is missing, regeneration won't happen. But if all goes well, you could have the tip of your finger back in about two months. Nail stem cells are being studied to see if they can be used to help regenerate other body parts—but for now, regrowing whole limbs remains a superhero specialty. Please take our word for it, and do *not* try this at home!

LOTS TO SMILE ABOUT

Behind the sweet smile of the adorable axolotl is the superpower to regrow many body parts: limbs, spinal cord, heart, even parts of the brain. When this Mexican salamander loses a limb, its blood clots right away and a special tissue called epithelium seals the wound. Then the severed nerves and epithelium prompt the creation of a blastema—a mass of cells that grows to form the new limb. Scientists are trying to figure out whether these same powers can be switched on in humans. They're also studying the axolotl's genome—a set of genetic instructions found in all living things. If scientists can figure out the specific genes responsible for regeneration, they may be able to find a way to increase the regenerative abilities in people. Researchers are also looking at other animal super-regenerators, including newts, planarian worms, African spiny mice, crabs, and deer!

– SECTION 2 –
SUPER FLIGHT

Do you know which superhero was the first to fly? Nope, not Superman! Back in October 1939, Namor the Sub-Mariner shot straight into the sky with the help of little (and scientifically impossible) wings on his ankles. Once airborne, he grabbed on to a plane to help his friend Dorma get away from some baddies.

Do you know another early flyer? Nope, still not Superman. Shazam (known as Captain Marvel then) took to the skies in June 1940. His power of flight was given to him by the immortal elder Mercury.

And let's not forget the heroes who can fly because they're from another world, like WordGirl from the planet Lexicon, who shoots into the air to battle supervillains and super-bad vocabulary.

Will humans ever be able to zoom through the sky like Namor, Shazam, or WordGirl? Unfortunately, it's just not possible. But that doesn't mean we'll always have to rely on airplanes, helicopters, or spacecraft either. Clever inventors have been working on autonomous human flight—meaning flying without an aircraft—for centuries. So while we'll never soar through the skies using just our bodies, by taking inspiration from E.X.O.'s power suit and the Rocketeer's jetpack, our flying days may not be so far off.

Off to a Flying Start

In Greek mythology, Daedalus built two pairs of wings out of wood, wax, and feathers so he and his son, Icarus, could escape the island where they were imprisoned. Daedalus warned Icarus to stay away from the sun. Icarus didn't listen, the wings melted, and he plummeted to a watery death. Daedalus made it to freedom. This is where the expression "Don't fly too close to the sun" comes from. It's a lesson about being reckless—and one that comes up repeatedly in humanity's pursuit of autonomous flight.

Timeline: HIGHLIGHTS (AND LOWLIGHTS) OF AUTONOMOUS HUMAN FLIGHT

Circa 875: In the part of Europe now known as Spain, Abbas Ibn Firnas builds glider-like wings using wood, silk, and eagle feathers. He flaps off a hill and is said to fly for a "considerable distance" before crash-landing. He survives but injures his back, blaming his accident on the lack of a tail. He's believed to be the first person to fly.

Circa 1630: Turkiye's Hezarfen Ahmed Çelebi builds himself "eagle wings," takes off from the top of a high tower, and reportedly flies 3.5 km (2.2 mi.) across the Bosporus Strait between Europe and Asia, making his first intercontinental flight.

1633: Lagari Hasan Çelebi, the brother of Hezarfen Çelebi, supposedly blasts 300 m (984 ft.) into the air and flies for twenty seconds in a human rocket pod—propelled by gunpowder!

2015: Canada's Catalin Alexandru Duru sets a world record for the farthest flight by hoverboard, at 275.9 m (905.2 ft.)—more than the length of two soccer fields. The hoverboard has propellers underneath and is controlled by Duru's feet, which are strapped into boots attached to the board.

1999: Inspired by de Gayardon's design, Finland's Jari Kuosma and Croatia's Robert Pečnik create the BIRDMAN s.u.i.t. Theirs is the first company to manufacture and sell wingsuits, and they also create a training course to teach others to use them.

1997: France's skydiving legend, Patrick de Gayardon, successfully debuts his modern-day ram-air wingsuit. Its wings inflate with the pressure of surrounding air to become semi-rigid.

1961: American engineer Harold Graham successfully lifts off for thirteen seconds using the Bell Aerosystems Rocket Belt, invented by engineer Wendell Moore. Although developed for the U.S. Army, the belt's short flying time and hydrogen peroxide fuel make it impractical for military use. Still, the belt causes a sensation when it's featured in the 1965 James Bond film *Thunderball*.

1954: France's Léo Valentin, known as the Birdman, jumps out of a plane and flies 4.8 km (3 mi.) using his rigid wooden wings. A paratrooper and parachute instructor—and perhaps the most famous daredevil to fly—the Birdman makes his last attempt at an air show in 1956. Tragically, the wood splinters, his parachutes don't open, and one hundred thousand horrified people watch as he plummets to his death.

1804: England's Sir George Cayley builds and flies a working glider that has wings and a tail. He publishes his studies in aerodynamics—the way wind moves around objects—five years later. He's considered the father of aviation.

Learning to Fly

For thousands of years, people have been attempting to fly like birds, but time and time again, the laws of physics have demonstrated that our bodies can't soar without some extra help.

WHY CAN'T WE JUST FLAP OUR ARMS?

Have you heard of strength-to-weight ratio? It's a quick calculation that lets you know how powerful your muscles are compared to your body weight. Just divide how much you can lift by what you weigh. Your number will probably be greater than your parents'. Even though you may not be as strong as they are, you likely weigh a lot less. That's why you can zip across the monkey bars and speed up a climbing wall while they dangle behind—it's easier for you to lift yourself up. Even so, your strength-to-weight ratio isn't as great as a bird's—if it was, you'd have a better chance at being able to fly. We humans just don't have enough strength in our arms or chests to lift our weight into the air and keep it off the ground. Birds, however, are built to fly, with light skeletons, hollow bones, and a powerful breathing system (they need only one breath for every two we take). And of course, they have wings, not arms!

PEDAL POWER

If we can't rely on our arms to fly, what about our legs? After all, our legs are at least three times stronger than our arms, and they're built for endurance. In 1988, the Massachusetts Institute of Technology (MIT), one of the top universities in the United States, built the Daedalus 88 (yep, named for Icarus's dad), a human-powered aircraft that had a 34 m (112 ft.) wingspan and weighed 31 kg (68 lb.). Greek Olympic cyclist Kanellos Kanellopoulos powered the 3 m (10 ft.) propellor by pedaling. He took off from the island of Crete (just like Daedalus and Icarus) and flew 119 km (74 mi.)—a flight that lasted three hours and fifty-four minutes! He had almost made it to Santorini, a neighboring island, when a strong headwind broke the aircraft. Thankfully, Kanellopoulos was able to swim to shore.

THE JET SET

One of the very first illustrations of a jetpack appeared on the August 1928 cover of *Amazing Stories* magazine: a man in a red suit hovers above the ground, waving to people below. One hundred years later, jetpacks still aren't commonly seen, even though some engineers are trying to make them so. A jetpack's engines propel the wearer by sucking in air that is then squeezed by a compressor, squirted with fuel, ignited, and shot out in the form of a burning-hot exhaust gas. Too dangerous? There's always the less flammable but still hazardous rocket belt, which combines hydrogen peroxide, pressurized liquid nitrogen, and a silver catalyst to blast steam out of its nozzles. Both options are based on the same idea: fuel → sparks → exhaust gas/steam → thrust = flight (+ DANGER). If that doesn't bother you, you still have to deal with the cost (high), the noise (loud), the flight time (short), and the aerodynamics (challenging).

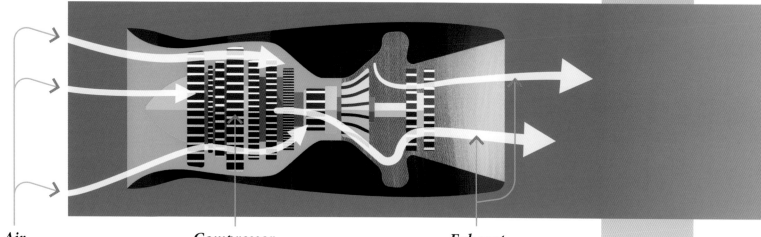

Air   *Compressor*   *Exhaust*

The Sky's the Limit

Humanity's desire to fly just won't quit. Our fascination with high-flying superheroes, such as Storm, Kagagi, and Green Lantern, is proof of that. Ingenious inventors are determined to help us take to the skies—whether it's using lightweight carbon wings or jet turbines.

WE HAVE LIFTOFF

Companies around the world are busy designing jetpacks and rocket belts to fly in the face of danger—with safety precautions in place, of course.

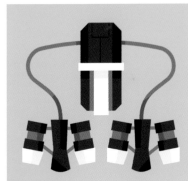

Rocket belts: Since 1975, Tecnologia Aeroespacial Mexicana founder and inventor Juan Manuel Lozano Gallegos has been working with hydrogen peroxide rocket engines. He started building his first rocket belt in the 1990s and lifted off in 2005. Two years later, he began selling belts customized according to the type of flight, weight of the wearer, fit, and more. He even sells a special machine so you can make your own hydrogen peroxide rocket fuel.

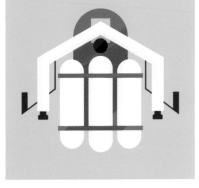

Jetpacks: David Mayman launched JetPack Aviation Corporation in 2016, not long after he completed an autonomous flight around New York's Statue of Liberty. His current model, the JB-11, features six turbo jet engines as well as a special computer that guides the pilot to safety in the case of engine failure.

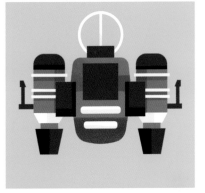

Jet suits: In 2017, inventor and former Royal Marine Richard Browning founded Gravity Industries to manufacture the Daedalus (that name again!) jet suit. Updated over the years, the current suit features two micro gas turbines on each arm and one turbine on the back. It also has a control system and a helmet with a display so the pilot can read fuel and engine data. Browning has been testing the suit for use with paramedic services and the British Royal Marines.

UP, UP, AND AWAY!

Soaring over the Swiss Alps. Circling Mt. Fuji. Flying across the Grand Canyon. Former military and commercial pilot Yves Rossy has done it all wearing a jet-propelled wing! In 2004, the Jetman, as Rossy is known, set a world record as the first person to fly horizontally using a jet wing. He jumped out of a plane, stayed airborne for four minutes, and then parachuted down to Earth. Back then, the Swiss inventor used a 3 m (10 ft.) lightweight carbon fiber wing with a jet engine at each end. He's been improving the wing's design ever since and has been experimenting with self-launching and self-landing—no plane needed!

UNDER PRESSURE

French jet ski racer and inventor Franky Zapata created the Flyboard Air, which has five jet engines that can reach speeds of 200 km/h (124 mph) and can fly for ten minutes at a time. The Flyboard Air comes after Zapata's success with water-powered designs: the original Flyboard soars vertically above the waves like Iron Man in his armor, while the Hoverboard moves horizontally like Silver Surfer on his board. Both are connected to superlong hoses that use the force from highly pressurized water to lift you into the air (as far as the hoses allow, of course).

– SECTION 3 –
SUPER SIGHT

Of all the powers Superman possesses, his X-ray vision seems to spark the most debate: scientists have studied whether it would really be possible, while others have wondered about the ethics of being able to see through almost *anything*. Sure, it's super useful to be able to scan a body for broken bones or pinpoint the exact location of bad guys in a hostage-taking situation, but could X-ray vision also cross a line into invasion of privacy? Hmm …

The power to go unseen has its pros and cons, too. While Nelvana of the Northern Lights uses her invisibility in the name of protecting the people of the North, those who aren't so righteous may choose to rob banks, spy, or worse, knowing they can't be identified.

Will science ever give us Superman-like X-ray vision? No. The high doses of radiation needed for the fictional superpower to actually work would likely cause cancer. But the good news is there are other forms of super vision in development, including smart lenses and bionic eyes.

And while we won't ever have the power of invisibility either, there are scientists experimenting with some pretty amazing ways to help us hide in plain sight. And who hasn't wanted to make like Violet Parr from *The Incredibles* and hide from the world every now and then?

At First Glance

How do our eyes work? A lot happens faster than you can say, "Kapow!" First, light bounces off an object, through your pupil, and to your lens. Then the lens focuses the light onto the retina at the back of your eye, which turns it into electrical signals that travel along your optic nerve. Your brain interprets those signals and—voilà!—you can see that object. Talk about powerful stuff!

Timeline: A HISTORY OF VISIONARY INVENTIONS

1021: Arab scholar Ibn al-Haytham publishes the *Book of Optics* and is the first to scientifically prove that we see because light bounces off visible objects and enters our eyes— rather than the long-debated belief that our eyes send rays of light. Ibn al-Haytham is considered the "father of modern optics."

1286: The first glasses are made by Italian monks who write religious texts. These scribes work at least six hours a day and need good eyesight.

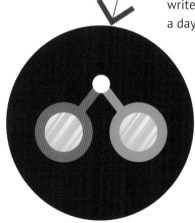

1608: Dutch eyeglass maker Hans Lippershey files a patent for the telescope. With two pieces of glass lined up, one concave (curving inward) for the eye and one convex (curving outward) for the lens, the telescope makes an object look three times its size.

2008: Canadian documentary filmmaker Rob Spence, who lost his right eye in a shotgun accident as a child, works on a custom-built prosthetic eye that records video. The prosthesis contains a video camera, a battery, and a transmitter. It's not connected to his optic nerve, so Spence uses it not to see but to record what's in his line of sight.

2003: Artist Neil Harbisson is fitted with an antenna that hangs over his head and a pair of headphones so he can hear color. The reason? He can see in black and white only. Today, the back of the antenna is attached to his skull and a chip turns light frequency into sound frequency, which is heard through the bones in his head.

1989: One of the first "wearable" computers, Private Eye has a mini computer screen worn over one eye and a vibrating mirror that projects content into the wearer's field of vision.

Mid-1930s: Germany develops night-vision technology, with the United States only steps behind. Infrared light is sent out and bounces back off an object to the night-vision device. Both countries use the technology during the Second World War.

1895: While German physicist Wilhelm Röntgen is conducting experiments with beams of electrons called cathode rays, a nearby screen begins to glow. Invisible rays had passed through a glass vacuum tube wrapped in thick black paper and onto the screen. Röntgen calls these mysterious rays "X-rays." Today we know that X-rays are a type of radiation in the electromagnetic spectrum.

See You on the Other Side

What you see is what you get, right? Not always! People working in science and technology are creating new ways for us to see through, see more, and see better.

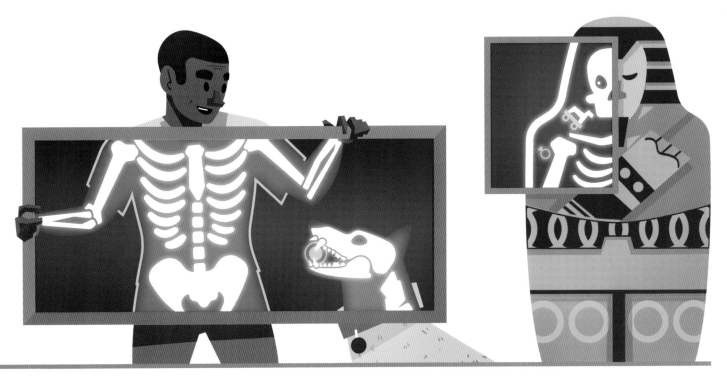

X MARKS THE SPOTS

When doctors take X-rays, some electromagnetic radiation rays are absorbed by hard materials, such as the calcium in your bones, while others pass through less dense tissue, like skin and lungs. But X-rays aren't only for doctors. Art historians use them to examine variations under finished paintings, archaeologists use them to see mummies inside ancient Egyptian sarcophagi, and security people use them to scan travelers' luggage at airports.

EYE SPY

Radio signals to the rescue! Although not as strong (or potentially harmful) as X-rays, radio-frequency (RF) radiation—the signals used in cellphones, Wi-Fi, Bluetooth, TV, and yes, radio—is also on the electromagnetic spectrum and can help us "see" through solid objects. An Israeli company called Camero has created a series of RF imaging devices that can detect movement through a wall, from even a football field away! This technology could be used to uncover earthquake survivors or expose an enemy ambush. By the way, blind superhero Daredevil also uses radio waves to "see" the outlines of what's around him.

A SIGHT FOR POOR EYES

For the world's 43 million blind people and 295 million people with moderate to severe visual impairments, bionic eyes might sound like a great option. But developing the technology is tricky because there are many different causes of low or no vision. And the way eyes and the brain communicate is also pretty complex. Current technology—such as special glasses that use a video camera to send signals to an implant on the retina, allowing the wearer to make out basic shapes and movement—tries to override the damaged part of the eye. But some researchers are working on bypassing the eye altogether with wireless implants that stimulate the visual cortex in the brain. Others are even testing a new high-tech eyeball—with better image resolution and night vision!

THE FUTURE'S IN SIGHT

Imagine seeing the weather forecast or sports scores with a blink of your eye. Tech companies around the world are racing to create "smart" lenses that do just that. One augmented reality contact lens in development, by a company called Mojo, projects information into the wearer's field of vision through a teeny tiny display built into the lens. (Augmented reality means adding to what you already see, while virtual reality replaces what you see.) One day soon, you may be able to use your eye movement to play music, zoom in on objects, and take pictures—which is getting awfully close to the powers of Cyborg's cybernetic eye. Oh, and these lenses would correct your vision, too.

Now You See It, Now You Don't

In the fictional world, characters like the Invisible Woman, the Vanisher, and Space Ghost use the power of invisibility to escape danger and listen in on supervillains' evil plans. Today, scientists and engineers are using their own superpowers to make invisibility a reality.

FADE INTO THE BACKGROUND

Scientists have developed all sorts of materials that can make people disappear—or seem to!

- In 2003, Japanese robotics and computer engineer Susumu Tachi introduced **retro-reflectum**, a cloaking material that allowed the wearer to blend into the background. It used a camera to project an image onto the cloak, but that meant the wearer couldn't move and was invisible only from one side.

- The media went into a frenzy in 2006 when British theoretical physicist John Pendry explained the science behind **metamaterials**, engineered materials that could bend light waves around an object to make the object look like it wasn't there. (Imagine light waves acting like water flowing around a rock in a stream and coming back together on the other side.)

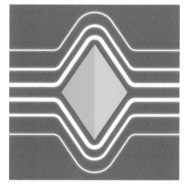

- In 2014, a team of scientists from MIT and Duke University in the US drew inspiration from under the sea. Much like an octopus blends into its surroundings, the team's **flexible polymer** material changes color and texture in response to an electrical current.

- Researchers in South Korea are developing an **artificial skin** made from pixelized patches that change color based on temperature. Also inspired by the sea, the patches would make the wearer invisible to the human eye and thermal-imaging cameras.

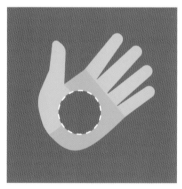

COLOR ME INVISIBLE

Rather than bend light waves, researchers in Montreal, Quebec, are trying to alter light's color with a spectral cloaking device. (The word "spectral" relates to the spectrum of light. It also means ghostly—which is fitting!) Although visible light looks white to the naked eye, it's actually made up of a variety of colors, each with its own light wavelength. When light shines on an object, some color wavelengths are reflected (the colors you see) and others are absorbed (the colors you don't). For example, a green jacket looks green because it reflects green wavelengths back to your eyes. But the cloaking device would alter that green wavelength so it gets absorbed by the jacket along with the other colors. No reflected green wavelength = no green jacket in sight!

VANISHING ACT

Your best bet at becoming invisible to the outside world? Stepping *inside* South Korea's Tower Infinity! The tower is covered with LED screens and cameras. The cameras capture what's happening on one side of the tower and project those images onto the screens on the opposite side. When the screens are on, people standing in certain spots outside will "see through" the tower—an optical camouflage! Because the screens are tilted down, it's only those on the ground who will experience the illusion—planes and birds flying head-on will still have the tower in view. The Tower Infinity, just outside Seoul, is slated to be finished in 2024. It's not exactly Wonder Woman's invisible plane, but it's pretty close.

– SECTION 4 –
SUPER STRENGTH

Some superheroes have acquired super strength through ill-fated or otherworldly means. Physicist Bruce Banner developed his angry alter-ego, the Hulk, after being exposed to gamma rays. Government agent Tom Evans was transformed into Captain Canuck after getting zapped with alien zeta rays while camping.

Other superheroes are ordinary people with extraordinary skills. There's hand-to-hand combat whiz Martha Washington, the highly skilled gymnast and athlete Black Widow, the martial arts master Shang-Chi, and of course, Batman, one of the most gifted and physically fit combatants around.

Physical strength is an important area of study for scientists. But they're not looking to recreate the out-of-this-world muscle power of Guardian Prime, who can stop an asteroid heading for Earth (though that could come in handy). Instead, they're researching ways to build and maintain muscle strength, including special fabrics, artificial muscle fibers, and exoskeleton suits. Our muscles do everything from keeping our blood pumping to forming a smile. We need our muscles to survive—period.

Of course, we know that strength isn't all about bulging muscles and powerful punches. You can also have strength of character—something you and your favorite superhero definitely have in common.

The Weight of the World

The human body has more than six hundred muscles! Our skeletal muscles are what help with lifting and movement. Made up of fibers or cells, they are attached to our bones by tendons and work in pairs, like the biceps and triceps in your upper arms. Our brain sends messages through the rest of our nervous system to activate the muscles. So much power under your control!

Timeline: A FEW LEGENDARY LIFTERS

Milo of Croton (Between 600 BCE and 500 BCE):
Considered the greatest wrestler of his day, Milo of Croton won medals at six Olympics and seven Pythian Games! It's said that the Greek athlete carried the same animal every day for years, from when it was a calf until it was a full-grown bull. Milo's method of gradually increasing weight is still the basis of training routines today.

Miss La La (1858 to unknown): Born Anna Olga Albertina Brown in a city that is now part of Poland, Miss La La gained fame in Paris for her astonishing strength and iron-jaw act. In one performance, she held a man in each arm and another using a special device clenched between her teeth—all while hanging from a trapeze with one leg! Her act was immortalized in a painting by famous French artist Edgar Degas.

Louis Cyr (1863 to 1912): Canadian Louis Cyr used his incredible strength to keep from being torn apart as two workhorses tied to his arms pulled with all their might. He also lifted a platform holding eighteen men, pushed a train car up a hill, lifted 243 kg (535 lb.) with his finger, and hoisted 860 kg (1,897 lb.) with two hands. It's no wonder Cyr is still considered the strongest man the world has ever known.

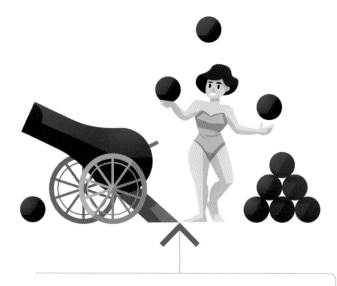

Charles Atlas (1892 to 1972): Born Angelo Siciliano in Italy and raised in the United States, Charles Atlas was a "97-pound weakling" who got sand kicked in his face and decided to remake himself so he would never be bullied again—a story that he used in his popular bodybuilding ads at the back of comic books. Atlas's Dynamic Tension system became the skinny boy's go-to, and Atlas himself became the face (and leopard-print-wearing body) of the ideal man.

The Great Sandwina (1884 to 1952):
Born Kathi Brumbach in Germany, the Great Sandwina worked for several circuses, impressing audiences with her ability to lift her husband above her head with one arm, bend iron bars, juggle cannonballs, and carry a cannon on her shoulders. If her stage name looks familiar, it should—rumor has it she got it after beating Eugen Sandow in a weightlifting exhibition!

Eugen Sandow (1867 to 1925):
Eugen Sandow is considered the father of modern bodybuilding. Born Friedrich Wilhelm Müller in a city that is now part of Russia, he toured the world showing off his impressive physique and strength. Sandow was the model for the Mr. Olympia bodybuilding trophy and trained famous people such as Sherlock Holmes author Arthur Conan Doyle.

Give Me Strength

You're stronger than you think! The average person uses no more than 65 percent of his or her full muscle power, while a trained weightlifter or elite athlete in competition can push that to around 90 percent. But our bodies actually keep us from using 100 percent because that can cause us physical harm. That said, scientists are constantly searching for ways to boost our everyday strength—safely.

HYSTERICAL STRENGTH

Can you lift a car? What if someone you love was stuck underneath it? People have shown seemingly impossible strength when faced with life-or-death situations. This is called hysterical strength, and it's a fight-or-flight reaction in which adrenaline is released to pump extra-oxygenated blood into our muscles, convert our stored energy into fuel, and raise our pain tolerance to give us emergency super strength. In fact, legendary comic book creator Jack Kirby came up with the Hulk after seeing a woman lift part of a car to save her son! While this is definitely incredible, scientists have discovered that producing too much adrenaline and other stress hormones for too long can cause serious health issues, like sleep disorders and depression.

THE ANATOMY OF A BODYBUILDER

How do bodybuilders get so ripped? Thanks to science, we now know! For years, people who wanted to build muscle believed the heavier the weight they lifted, the bigger their muscles would get. But physiologists—scientists who study how the different parts of living things work—have shown that while weight is important, so is the quality of the repetitions. (A repetition is a strength-training exercise that is repeated. For example, one bicep curl is one repetition.) To make each repetition count, you need to slow the movement down. The longer the muscles are under tension, the harder they work and the bigger they'll grow!

TRAIN, SLEEP, REPEAT

Physiologists also discovered that when you want to increase muscle, short and intense training targeting different muscle groups on different days is better than working out the whole body in one go. It's also better to do sets (a specific number of repetitions before taking a quick break) at one level of resistance (weight) and gradually increase that resistance over time. (Remember Milo of Croton and the growing calf?) Bodybuilders know that getting plenty of rest between workouts is also important. When you sleep, your body releases growth hormones that repair any little tears in your muscles from that day, making your muscles stronger.

UNFAIR ADVANTAGE

Anabolic steroids were first created in the 1930s and used to treat depression and other medical and psychiatric issues. Today they're used to help with delayed puberty, breast cancer, and other conditions. But since the 1952 Olympics, some athletes have taken them to bulk up and improve their results. These performance-enhancing drugs are artificial forms of testosterone, a hormone that males and, to a lesser extent, females make naturally. Anabolic steroids are banned in sports—taking them gives competitors an unfair advantage over athletes who have trained hard to become naturally strong, fit, and fast. They can also have negative side effects, from severe acne to aggressive behavior to heart problems.

Coming on Strong

Scientists are studying the animal kingdom for ideas on how to make humans stronger. From futuristic fabrics and tough skeletons to artificial muscles, their discoveries pack a powerful punch.

SLIME TIME

Hagfish are pretty gross. The eel-like fish have two rows of pointy "teeth" that let them tear open dead prey, worm their way inside, and feast. Lovely. But these scavengers may be the future of fabric. When hagfish are under attack, they pump out a couple of key ingredients that combine with seawater to expand into a slime. That slime eventually chokes the predator, giving the hagfish enough time to get away. But here's the thing: the slime is made up of long, thin threads that become super strong and stretchy when dry. Researchers think these protein threads are the key to creating a renewable, eco-friendly material that could one day be used to make Black Panther–like bulletproof armor, protective sprays that navy divers can release like Spider-Man's webs when faced with danger, and more.

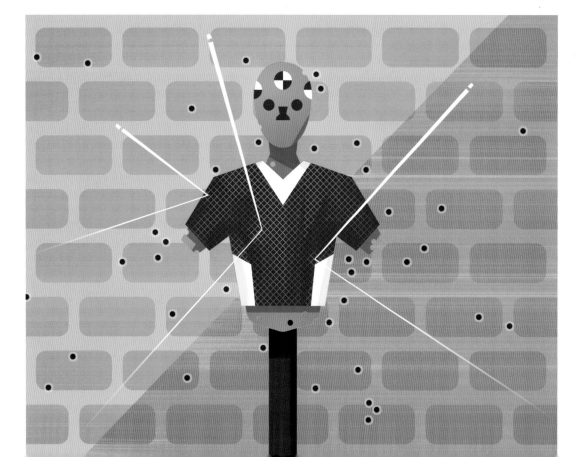

WHAT'S YOUR STRONG SUIT?

Lots of animals, including scorpions, lobsters, earwigs, and the awesomely named diabolical ironclad beetle, have protective exoskeletons—skeletons that are on the outside of their bodies. Today, thanks to scientists and engineers, people can have them, too. Wearable exoskeletons are sometimes called exosuits. Some are a hard shell made of metal or carbon fiber and worn over your clothes, while others are made of a lightweight material and worn under your clothes. Exosuits provide strength and support with artificial muscles that are powered by batteries, electricity, or human movement. They can be used to help people with mobility issues learn to move again, to make it easier to lift and carry super-heavy things on construction sites, to prevent injury in sports such as downhill skiing, and to make soldiers stronger and faster.

LET'S DO THE TWIST

Our skeletal muscles are made up of hundreds to thousands of bundled muscle fibers that work together to help us move. To make artificial muscle fibers that can potentially be used in lightweight exoskeletons and prostheses, researchers have been testing and twisting different kinds of inexpensive fibers (such as bamboo, silk, and nylon), coating them with a polymer to make a sock-like covering, and then twisting them again into coils. When heated, the fibers contract like real muscles—but deliver way more strength!

– SECTION 5 –
SUPER BRAINS

When we think of mind control, we tend to think of villains who take over people's thoughts, making them do terrible, nefarious things. But there are those who use their mind-grabbing gift for good, like *The Umbrella Academy*'s Allison Hargreeves. All she has to do is begin a sentence with "I heard a rumor," add an action she wants, like getting bad guys to turn on each other, and—boom!—done. There's also *My Hero Academia*'s Hitoshi Shinso, who can brainwash anyone within hearing distance who replies to him. Although people doubt his intentions, he just wants to save lives.

So is it actually possible to take over someone else's mind? In a manner of speaking, yes. Brainwashing is the use of persuasion techniques to manipulate another person into changing her thoughts, ideas, beliefs, or actions. There's also hypnosis, in which a therapist or other practitioner taps into a person's subconscious to make suggestions.

Our brains are complex and fascinating organs that scientists are still trying to fully understand. With each step forward, they are finding ways of using our own brainpower to improve memory, reduce physical pain, and treat mental health. They are even looking at the possibility of telepathy—the ability to communicate mind to mind, like X-Men's Jean Grey and Professor X are able to do. But when it comes to telekinesis—that mind-over-matter superhero power belonging to Martian Manhunter and the Scarlet Witch—well, scientists remain skeptical.

A Thought-Provoking Past

For hundreds of years, doctors and scientists—working on their own or for government agencies—have experimented with hypnosis, conditioning, brainwashing, and brain stimulation to control or change people's behavior.

Timeline: A BRIEF HISTORY OF MIND-BLOWING INNOVATIONS

1770s: German physician Franz Anton Mesmer claims he can cure illness through an invisible force called animal magnetism. In Paris, he convinces French society of his talents, transferring the "force" from his hands while putting patients into a trancelike state (later known as mesmerism). A doubtful King Louis XVI has a team investigate. It turns out that Mesmer's patients *are* being cured—not by Mesmer but by their belief in his power. In other words, by the power of suggestion. Still, Mesmer is considered one of the creators of hypnosis.

1890s: Russian physiologist Ivan Pavlov begins testing a theory about learned behavior. Having observed that his lab dogs automatically drool when their food comes, Pavlov starts a metronome as the food arrives. By doing this over and over, he trains the dogs to associate the sound of the metronome with being fed. Eventually, Pavlov starts the metronome and the dogs drool, even with no food in sight! He calls this a conditional reflex. People can also be conditioned to react or behave a certain way—and counter-conditioned to overcome fears and anxiety.

1963: Spanish neuroscientist José Delgado stops a bull charging toward him with just the push of a button on a handheld radio transmitter! The button sends electrical stimulation through an implant in the bull's brain to control its aggressive behavior. Delgado's work on humans shows that terrible pain can be made better or epileptic seizures prevented through brain stimulation. His pioneering work continues today as scientists explore deep brain stimulation to improve the lives of those with certain neurological and mental-health conditions.

1953: Fearing that communist countries have already developed ways to control minds, the US Central Intelligence Agency (CIA) launches a secret mind-control program called Project MK-Ultra. Its goal is to create a truth serum, an amnesiac to induce memory loss, and a method of controlling agents' actions without their knowing. As part of the testing, many unsuspecting volunteers, patients, and prisoners are subjected to mind-altering drugs, electroshock, hypnotism, sensory deprivation, and repeated recorded messages. The program continues until 1963, with no success.

1950: The term "brainwashing"—from the Mandarin words *xǐ nǎo*, meaning "wash" and "brain"—is first used in printed English when a newspaper article claims the Chinese government is controlling the minds of its citizens through various means, including drugs and hypnotism. This would later prove to be untrue.

The Power to Control Others

We've all heard that our minds can play tricks on us, but a scientific understanding of our brains shows us that we can also play tricks on our minds, from thought manipulation to the power of persuasion.

HOW DOES BRAINWASHING WORK?

In the fictional world, brainwashing is a super-villainous technique used by evil organizations such as Marvel's Hydra to turn soldiers like Bucky Barnes into assassins. Similar techniques have been used in the real world, too. Most commonly, a charming leader obtains a person's loyalty and obedience through techniques such as sleep and food deprivation, reward and punishment, and isolation from friends and family. This treatment weakens people psychologically, making them vulnerable to having their thoughts manipulated by repeated messaging and new ideas.

YOU'RE GETTING SLEEPY...

When you hear the word "hypnotist," you might imagine a person swinging a gold pocket watch and putting someone into a trancelike state to make them do something embarrassing, like cluck like a chicken. Or maybe you think of a supervillain like Doctor Psycho or Mesmero. But hypnosis is also used for good by the likes of the Shadow—and by trained therapists! So what exactly is hypnosis? It's a state in which a person is relaxed, aware, suggestible, *and* in control. By tapping into a person's subconscious and using the power of suggestion, hypnotherapists can help reduce pain and anxiety and change unhealthy behaviors, such as smoking and overeating. The practice is not without controversy; some worry about what an unscrupulous hypnotherapist could do, like force a person to do something they normally wouldn't. With hypnotherapy, the only mind control should be the patient telling their own unhealthy thoughts to take a hike.

MIND-BENDING ACTS

To be telekinetic—able to move objects with your mind—you'd have to have
the power to break the unbreakable laws of physics. Though many people have
claimed to have such power, researchers are still waiting for actual undeniable
evidence. So far, any claims of telekinesis have been revealed as tricks or simply
explained away. But why do these acts often seem so real? Our thoughts have
been expertly influenced or guided by the performer, and so we believe.
This is the power of suggestion, which is also the basis for mesmerism
(remember that guy?) and magic tricks.

Forward Thinking

Talk about mind-blowing! One day, we may be able to speak, compose music, and write essays without opening our mouths or even lifting a finger. Scientists are working on revolutionary ways to harness the power of our minds to communicate using thought alone.

MUSIC OF THE MIND

In 2020, a Canadian musician with a background in neuroscience created music with her mind. Wearing a headset that read her brain's electrical activity, Angie Coombes thought of different words and images, and those were immediately translated by special software and sent to The Original New Timbral Orchestra (TONTO), a one-of-a-kind music synthesizer, to produce a variety of sounds. Coombes's emotion-driven signals controlled the music's volume, reverb, and pitch. She even recorded parts of a new album this way. The experiment was a world first!

DON'T SAY IT, CONVEY IT!

Researchers at the MIT Media Lab in the United States are working on a wearable device that can read signals from your facial and vocal cord muscles—signals made just before you open your mouth to speak. The device sends these signals to your computer and sends back any audio reply using bone conduction headphones. (These bonephones bypass your eardrums by sending sound vibrations through bones in your head directly to your cochlea, which contains the sensory organ of hearing, so only you can hear them.) The device would allow users to send messages, translate languages, and overcome speech disorders. And don't worry—you have to intentionally form the words you want to convey, so your deepest thoughts won't be revealed!

I KNOW WHAT YOU'RE THINKING

Telepathy—the transfer of thoughts from one person to another—may be here sooner than you think. Scientists are developing technologies that might allow non-speaking people to communicate with loved ones, or military leaders to secretly send commands to their troops. The devices might even let you compose a school essay just by thinking it up! Here's how they could work:

Brain-to-Computer Interface (BCI): This transfers thoughts from a person's brain to a computer, which then turns them into an action. Neural signals are read by electrodes implanted in the brain or by an electroencephalography (EEG) headset.

Brain-to-Brain Interface (BBI): This transfers thoughts from one person's brain directly to another's. There are two methods, both of which use a computer to process the message from the sender and relay it to the receiver. In the first method, electrodes are implanted in both brains to read neural signals and fire specific neurons. In the second, one person wears an EEG headset that sends neural signals to another person, who receives the information through a device on their head that stimulates specific neurons.

– SECTION 6 –
SUPER SURVIVAL

Some superheroes have a power that allows them to walk into battle without worry, knowing if they're killed, their death can be reversed and they will live forever. But is their immortality awesome or actually awful?

Think about it. How many thousands of years more can the aptly named Immortal keep losing friends and loved ones before he just can't take it anymore? What will life be like for *The Umbrella Academy*'s Klaus Hargreeves (immortal because neither heaven nor hell wants him) when he is the only one left after his sisters and brothers pass away, even if he can talk to the dead?

Here's a question for us regular humans: Is death the sure thing we've always thought it to be? Reanimation, revival, resuscitation, rebirth, resurrection—call it what you want, but people have been fascinated by the idea of defying death probably since life began. Though the medical world generally considers a brain-dead body to be dead, that hasn't stopped some from trying to get the body going again. Or from freezing dying people so their health issues can be healed at a later time. Or from transforming loved ones into digital doubles.

Death is hard. But is living forever really better? Some scientists seem to think so.

1732: Scottish surgeon William Tossach literally breathes life into suffocated coal miner James Blair, who—with no pulse, cold skin, and staring eyes—is "in all appearance dead." Blair's recovery is considered the first clinically recorded description of mouth-to-mouth resuscitation.

Timeline:
DEATH-DEFYING MOMENTS

1803: Italian physicist (and Galvani's nephew) Giovanni Aldini takes Galvanism even further—by testing it on humans. Most famously, he sends electric shocks through a convict's corpse, making the body jerk about and an eye pop open—all in front of an audience! Aldini's work leads the way for electrotherapy and deep brain stimulation.

1786: Reanimation is accidentally discovered by Italian physician Luigi Galvani when an electrified scalpel makes a dead frog's legs twitch. Galvani theorizes that an electrical charge—even lightning—can make muscles contract, and that living creatures must have "animal electricity." His work, which came to be known as Galvanism, inspires the field of electrophysiology, the creation of pacemakers, and Mary Shelley's *Frankenstein*, one of the most famous stories about reanimation ever.

A Matter of Life and Death

By the late 1700s, people were so worried about having an "apparent death"—meaning thought to be dead but not actually dead—that safety coffins were invented. These had features like a bell that the buried-but-not-dead person could ring to signal for help. Is it such a far-fetched idea to come back to life after death? Scientists have been pondering that question for centuries.

1925: Russian physician and scientist Sergei Brukhonenko keeps the severed head of a dog alive for a couple of hours with his autojector device, which allows blood to stay warm and circulate. Brukhonenko believes his invention, one of the first heart-lung machines, could be used to keep the heart alive during operations and to resuscitate the dead. His work is considered an important step in cardiac surgery.

1934: American scientist Robert E. Cornish allegedly brings a dog named Lazarus IV back to life. He repeats the experiment successfully with Lazarus V in 1935. How? By strapping the fresh corpse of each dog to a seesaw-like board and rocking it back and forth to get the blood flowing while injecting the body with a concoction of stimulants. Cornish asks three American states to provide him with the bodies of dead convicts so he can try resuscitating a human. All three states say no.

1960: Almost 230 years after Tossach revived Blair, cardiopulmonary resuscitation (CPR) is invented. CPR combines mouth-to-mouth breathing and chest compressions, and it can sometimes revive a person from clinical death, which means there's no heartbeat and no breathing, but the patient hasn't yet been declared biologically dead.

1982: The Lazarus phenomenon, in which people come back to life on their own, is first recorded. A rare occurrence, it happens when a person's blood circulation spontaneously returns after CPR has been stopped—even as much as ten to fifteen minutes later. (One person was already in the mortuary!) Some survivors have gone on to fully recover, but roughly two-thirds died—again!—soon after.

A New Lease on Life

We can perform CPR to restart a heart that's stopped beating. We can hook people up to a ventilator when their lungs have failed. We can make life by cloning sheep and deer. But can we use technology to regenerate a dead brain and therefore a dead body?
More importantly, should we?

DEEP FREEZE

When Captain America's plane went down in 1945, the soldier survived the crash but froze in the Arctic ice. When he was discovered decades later, he hadn't changed a bit. Cryonics is a similar real-life idea: dead patients are cooled to super-low temperatures so they can one day be revived and treated for whatever killed them in the first place. So far, no human has been restored to life through this process. But plenty of frozen hopefuls await, including Dr. James Bedford, who, in 1967, was the first person ever to be cryonically preserved; writer and editor Du Hong (she only had her brain frozen); and baseball legend Ted Williams. Despite rumors, Walt Disney is not among them.

WHEN IS DEAD REALLY DEAD?

Scientists have long believed that once a living being dies, the brain cells quickly follow. But in 2019, researchers at Yale University in the United States discovered that some brain cells of a pig that had been dead for hours could start working again. The researchers were quick to point out that a "cellularly active brain" is not the same thing as a "living brain," which shows signs of consciousness, awareness, and other electrical activity. So why does any of this matter? The research could lead to further discoveries that help those who have suffered strokes or are experiencing other brain-related issues. But it also leaves scientists questioning when dead is actually dead, and whether it might be possible to one day fully restore a brain to consciousness.

DIGITAL DARLINGS

If we can't reanimate the dead, what about keeping them forever in digital form? In a 2020 documentary, a mother in South Korea strapped on a virtual reality headset to "meet" with an avatar form of her seven-year-old deceased daughter. Some people have built chatbots—artificial intelligence software that interacts with a living person through text or speech—to continue "speaking" with their loved ones. Others are researching the possibility of using information compiled from a person's digital footprint to create personality-driven avatars that can interact and even offer advice. Digital is one way to go, but there are other ways to achieve immortality: by donating your organs when you die so others can live and by being remembered by your loved ones.

Conclusion

From the Cairo toe dating back to 950 BCE to brain-to-computer interfaces being developed now, we have long sought ways to improve our physical bodies and the way they perform. Thanks to science and innovation, today we can replace two-thirds of the human body with artificial parts, fly around tall mountains with a jetpack, see through earthquake rubble to find survivors using radio signals, lift heavy materials while wearing an exosuit, relieve pain by talking to the subconscious mind, and revive the clinically dead through CPR.

There are some who believe we should go even further and use all the technology at our disposal to make our minds and bodies even better. They believe that no one should die from old age or disease because technology can replace whatever is failing. Imagine if everything you've read in this book is brought together into one person!

The super enhancements you've read about here may be carried out on our bodies, but they also have an effect on our moral code. In other words, is what we're accomplishing right or wrong? Will we know when we've crossed the line between doing good and going too far? And who draws that line, anyway?

While the Yale researchers who studied the dead pig's brain cells weren't willing to let any form of consciousness return to their test subject, Robert E. Cornish didn't seem to have any concern about testing reanimation on dead convicts. While many athletes follow the latest science to build their strength by training for years upon years, there are those who take a dangerous shortcut by popping performance-enhancing drugs. Just because we can do something, does that mean we should?

As real-world technology advances, we seem to be gaining at least some of the powers of our favorite superheroes. Is there a future where we will heal instantly, fly autonomously, and live forever? Based on everything we know right now, we may want to seriously start considering that ultimate superhero decision: Cape or no cape?

SELECTED BIBLIOGRAPHY

General

Cowsill, Alan, Alex Irvine, Steve Korte, Matt Manning, Stephen (Win) Wiacek, and Sven Wilson. *The DC Comics Encyclopedia: The Definitive Guide to the Characters of the DC Universe.* New York: Dorling Kindersley, 2016.

Nicholson, Hope. *The Spectacular Sisterhood of Superwomen: Awesome Female Characters from Comic Book History.* Philadelphia: Quirk Books, 2017.

Wiacek, Stephen. *The Marvel Book: Expand Your Knowledge of a Vast Comics Universe.* New York: Dorling Kindersley, 2019.

Super Parts

Brumfiel, Geoff. "The Insane and Exciting Future of the Bionic Body." *Smithsonian Magazine*, September 2013. Online.

Murphy, Wendy B. *Spare Parts: From Peg Legs to Gene Splices.* Brookfield, CN: Twenty-First Century Books, 2001.

Science Museum Group. "Search Our Collection." Online.

Super Flight

Abrams, Michael. *Birdmen, Batmen, and Skyflyers: Wingsuits and the Pioneers Who Flew in Them, Fell in Them, and Perfected Them.* New York: Harmony Books, 2006.

Lehto, Steve. *The Great American Jet Pack: The Quest for the Ultimate Individual Lift Device.* Chicago: Chicago Review Press, 2013.

Super Sight

Emslie, Karen. "10 Bizarre, Vision-Enhancing Technologies from the Last 1,000 Years." *Smithsonian Magazine*, April 13, 2016. Online.

NASA Science. "Tour of the Electromagnetic Spectrum." Online.

Super Strength

Hadhazy, Adam. "How It's Possible for an Ordinary Person to Lift a Car." BBC Future, May 1, 2016. Online.

DKfindout! "Muscles." Online.

Super Brains

Boissoneault, Lorraine. "The True Story of Brainwashing and How It Shaped America." *Smithsonian Magazine*, May 22, 2017. Online.

Hammer, A. Gordon, and Martin T. Orne. "Hypnosis." *Encyclopaedia Britannica*, last updated August 15, 2021. Online.

Super Survival

Fantastic Worlds: Science and Fiction 1780–1910. "The Body Electric." Smithsonian Libraries and Archives. Online.

Manley, Janet. "The Ethics of Rebooting the Dead." *Wired*, November 26, 2020. Online.

GLOSSARY

aerodynamics: The study of the four forces of flight—thrust, drag, lift, and weight—and the way wind moves around objects.

artificial intelligence (AI): The ability of technology, or smart machines, to think and act like human beings.

augmented reality: Overlaying digital information to what you currently see in the real world.

brainwashing: The use of persuasion techniques to manipulate people into changing their thoughts, beliefs, or actions.

chatbot: Artificial intelligence software that interacts through text or speech with a living person.

cryonics: The practice of storing of dead people at super-low temperatures in hopes of one day reviving them and allowing them to live on.

cybernetic: The combining of body and machine. Cybernetic + organism = cyborg.

digital footprint: The trail of information about a person left online because of web-based activities, like posting to social media.

electroencephalography (EEG): A test in which electrodes are placed against the scalp to read the brain's electrical activity.

genome: A body's complete set of genetic instructions.

hypnotherapy: Therapist-led hypnosis. Used to tap into a person's subconscious to help treat mental or physical health issues and change harmful behaviors.

muscle graft: Healthy muscle that is transplanted from one part of the body to another.

polymer: A substance made of a repeating pattern of linking molecules, like plastic, nylon, and even your DNA.

pupil: The black circle in the center of the eye where light enters.

regeneration: The ability to regrow a body part that has been damaged or removed.

residual limb: The part of an arm or leg a person still has after amputation of the rest.

stem cells: Basic cells in your body that can become different kinds of specialized cells, like a nerve or brain cell.

telekinesis: The power to move objects with your mind.

telepathy: Mind-to-mind communication.

thrust: An aerodynamic force that pushes an object forward.

virtual reality: Immersion in a three-dimensional, computer-created world through special devices, like a VR headset.

visible light: The part of the electromagnetic spectrum that can be seen with the human eye.

wavelength: The distance between two corresponding points of a light wave, like peak to peak. Each color has a different wavelength; of visible colors, red has the longest and violet the shortest.

X-ray: A type of radiation wave in the electromagnetic spectrum.